Frequently Misspelled Words
6th grade to 8th grade

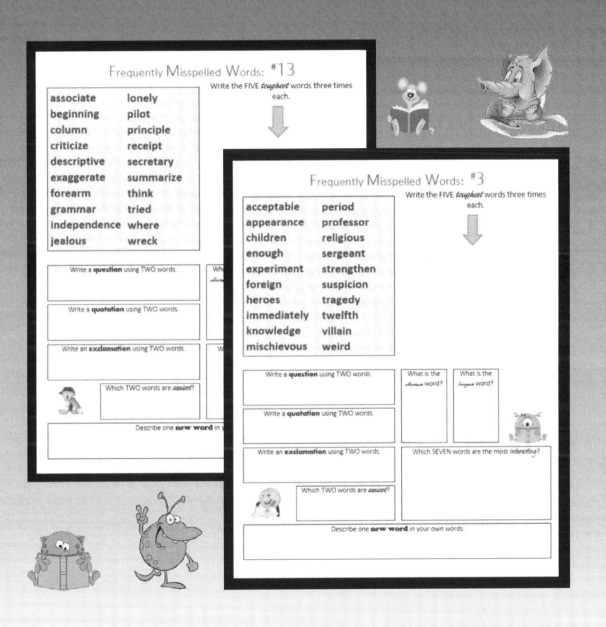

Frequently Misspelled Words: #13

associate	lonely
beginning	pilot
column	principle
criticize	receipt
descriptive	secretary
exaggerate	summarize
forearm	think
grammar	tried
independence	where
jealous	wreck

Write the FIVE *toughest* words three times each.

Write a **question** using TWO words.

Write a **quotation** using TWO words.

Write an **exclamation** using TWO words.

Which TWO words are *easiest*?

Describe one **new word** in...

Frequently Misspelled Words: #3

acceptable	period
appearance	professor
children	religious
enough	sergeant
experiment	strengthen
foreign	suspicion
heroes	tragedy
immediately	twelfth
knowledge	villain
mischievous	weird

Write the FIVE *toughest* words three times each.

Write a **question** using TWO words.

What is the *shortest* word?

What is the *longest* word?

Write a **quotation** using TWO words.

Write an **exclamation** using TWO words.

Which SEVEN words are the most *interesting*?

Which TWO words are *easiest*?

Describe one **new word** in your own words.

by C. Mahoney

Life is about choices...

Contents

20 sets of printable handouts. Each set has twenty words and four options:

First option: Students respond to nine directives: toughest and easiest words, shortest and longest words, new or interesting words, use words in a question or exclamation or quotation, and practice.

Second option: Students can practice their words, or write sentences using the words, or explain why these twenty words are frequently misspelled.

Third option: Students hide ten of the toughest words in a word search and write a funny story using five words.

Fourth option: Students practice the ten toughest (thrice) and five easiest words (once), write three questions and three exclamations, and compose three silly sentences.

The 400 words in these twenty lists came from two sources. You can find both online by Googling their title and "pdf". Both are research-based.

#1: *Words Most Frequently Misspelled by High School Students*
A study published in *The English Journal* in October 1971 showed that 1.5% of the words used by students in grades 9–12 accounted for 28% of the misspellings. Just 6% of the words accounted for 51% of the misspellings! The 388 words which accounted for over half of the misspellings are listed below, in order of frequency of misspelling. [I include this list for middle schoolers, grades 6-8, to help you give your students a leg up on their fellow high schoolers.]

#2: The *100 Most Misspelled Words in the English Language* compiled by yourdictionary.com. [I have found numerous lists online that contain about 80% of the same words, with about 20% variation. Words like vacuum, thief, receive and others are on every list because students frequently misspell them and many don't seem to follow an established or known rule.]

Frequently Misspelled Words: #1

accuse	interpret
address	leisure
all right	obstacle
amateur	physical
cemetery	prison
completely	quantity
enough	remember
escape	shepherd
February	tomorrow
further	wonderful

Write the FIVE *toughest* words three times each.

Write a **question** using TWO words.

Write a **quotation** using TWO words.

Write an **exclamation** using TWO words.

What is the *shortest* word?

What is the *longest* word?

Which SEVEN words are the most *interesting*?

Which TWO words are *easiest*?

Describe one **new word** in your own words.

Frequently Misspelled Words: #1

accuse	interpret
address	leisure
all right	obstacle
amateur	physical
cemetery	prison
completely	quantity
enough	remember
escape	shepherd
February	tomorrow
further	wonderful

Frequently Misspelled Words: #1

accuse	completely	interpret	quantity
address	enough	leisure	remember
all right	escape	obstacle	shepherd
amateur	February	physical	tomorrow
cemetery	further	prison	wonderful

Hide the TEN toughest words in this word search

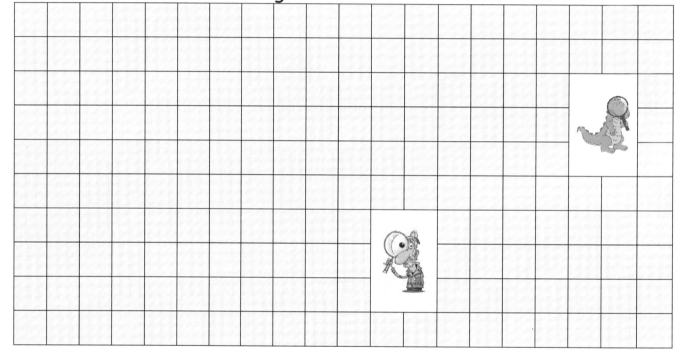

Write a funny story using FIVE of these words.

_____

_____

_____

_____

_____

_____

_____

Frequently Misspelled Words: #1

accuse	completely	interpret	quantity
address	enough	leisure	remember
all right	escape	obstacle	shepherd
amateur	February	physical	tomorrow
cemetery	further	prison	wonderful

Write the TEN **easiest** words once.

Write the FIVE **toughest** words thrice.

Create **questions** (<u>underline</u> your words).

1.

2.

3.

Create **exclamations** (<u>underline</u> your words).

1.

2.

3.

Write three silly sentences using TWO different words in each.

1.

2.

3.

Frequently Misspelled Words: #2

accidentally	fictitious
argument	gauge
beautiful	guarantee
brilliance	happily
conscience	identify
curiosity	ignorance
difference	maintenance
effect	nervous
especially	pastime
familiar	poison

Write the FIVE *toughest* words three times each.

Write a **question** using TWO words.

Write a **quotation** using TWO words.

Write an **exclamation** using TWO words.

Which TWO words are *easiest*?

What is the *shortest* word?

What is the *longest* word?

Which SEVEN words are the most *interesting*?

Describe one **new word** in your own words.

accidentally	fictitious
argument	gauge
beautiful	guarantee
brilliance	happily
conscience	identify
curiosity	ignorance
difference	maintenance
effect	nervous
especially	pastime
familiar	poison

Frequently Misspelled Words: #2

accidentally	curiosity	fictitious	ignorance
argument	difference	gauge	maintenance
beautiful	effect	guarantee	nervous
brilliance	especially	happily	pastime
conscience	familiar	identify	poison

Hide the TEN toughest words in this word search

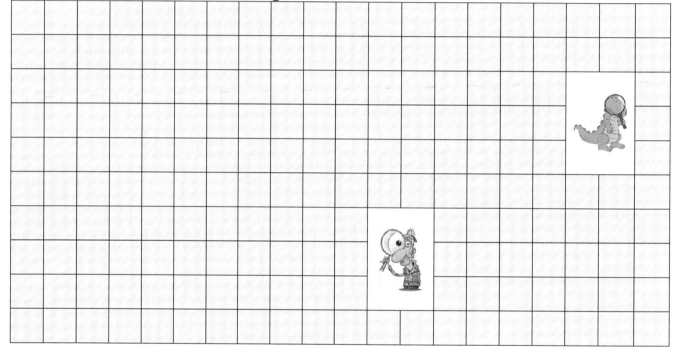

Write a funny story using FIVE of these words.

_____

_____

_____

_____

_____

_____

_____

_____

Frequently Misspelled Words: #2

accidentally	curiosity	fictitious	ignorance
argument	difference	gauge	maintenance
beautiful	effect	guarantee	nervous
brilliance	especially	happily	pastime
conscience	familiar	identify	poison

Write the TEN **easiest** words once.

Write the FIVE **toughest** words thrice.

Create **questions** (<u>underline</u> your words).

1.

2.

3.

Create **exclamations** (<u>underline</u> your words).

1.

2.

3.

Write three silly sentences using TWO different words in each.

1.

2.

3.

Frequently Misspelled Words: #3

acceptable	period
appearance	professor
children	religious
enough	sergeant
experiment	strengthen
foreign	suspicion
heroes	tragedy
immediately	twelfth
knowledge	villain
mischievous	weird

Write the FIVE *toughest* words three times each.

Write a **question** using TWO words.

Write a **quotation** using TWO words.

Write an **exclamation** using TWO words.

Which TWO words are *easiest*?

What is the *shortest* word?

What is the *longest* word?

Which SEVEN words are the most *interesting*?

Describe one **new word** in your own words.

Frequently Misspelled Words: #3

acceptable	period
appearance	professor
children	religious
enough	sergeant
experiment	strengthen
foreign	suspicion
heroes	tragedy
immediately	twelfth
knowledge	villain
mischievous	weird

Frequently Misspelled Words: #3

acceptable	foreign	period	suspicion
appearance	heroes	professor	tragedy
children	immediately	religious	twelfth
enough	knowledge	sergeant	villain
experiment	mischievous	strengthen	weird

Hide the TEN toughest words in this word search

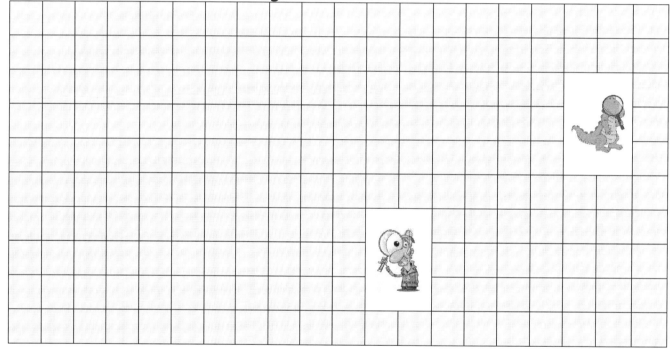

Write a funny story using FIVE of these words.

_____

_____

_____

_____

_____

_____

_____

_____

Frequently Misspelled Words: #3

acceptable	foreign	period	suspicion
appearance	heroes	professor	tragedy
children	immediately	religious	twelfth
enough	knowledge	sergeant	villain
experiment	mischievous	strengthen	weird

Write the TEN **easiest** words once.

Write the FIVE **toughest** words thrice.

Create **questions** (underline your words).

1.

2.

3.

Create **exclamations** (underline your words).

1.

2.

3.

Write three silly sentences using TWO different words in each.

1.

2.

3.

Frequently Misspelled Words: #4

afraid	peculiar
because	psychology
changeable	rhythm
courageous	soldier
discipline	sophomore
excellent	supersede
friend	their
intelligence	tyranny
meant	wonder
ninety	you're

Write the FIVE *toughest* words three times each.

Write a **question** using TWO words.

Write a **quotation** using TWO words.

Write an **exclamation** using TWO words.

Which TWO words are *easiest*?

What is the *shortest* word?

What is the *longest* word?

Which SEVEN words are the most *interesting*?

Describe one **new word** in your own words.

afraid	peculiar
because	psychology
changeable	rhythm
courageous	soldier
discipline	sophomore
excellent	supersede
friend	their
intelligence	tyranny
meant	wonder
ninety	you're

Frequently Misspelled Words: #4

afraid	excellent	peculiar	supersede
because	friend	psychology	their
changeable	intelligence	rhythm	tyranny
courageous	meant	soldier	wonder
discipline	ninety	sophomore	you're

Hide the TEN toughest words in this word search

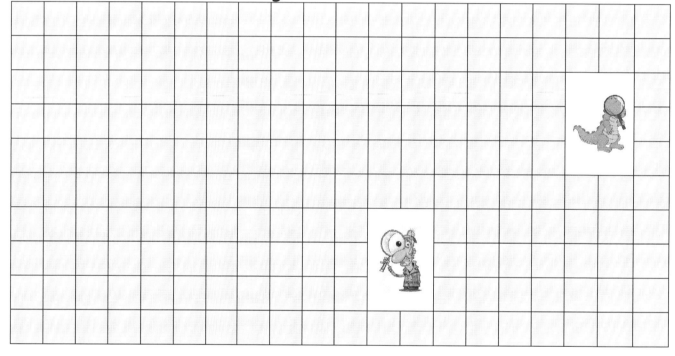

Write a funny story using FIVE of these words.

_____

_____

_____

_____

_____

_____

_____

Frequently Misspelled Words: #4

afraid	excellent	peculiar	supersede
because	friend	psychology	their
changeable	intelligence	rhythm	tyranny
courageous	meant	soldier	wonder
discipline	ninety	sophomore	you're

Write the TEN **easiest** words once.

Write the FIVE **toughest** words thrice.

Create **questions** (<u>underline</u> your words).

1.

2.

3.

Create **exclamations** (<u>underline</u> your words).

1.

2.

3.

Write three silly sentences using TWO different words in each.

1.

2.

3.

Frequently Misspelled Words: #5

acquaint	hierarchy
aggression	interesting
athletic	library
bicycle	minute
chief	occurrence
destroy	piece
embarrass	prejudice
exciting	quiet
field	relief
guard	search

Write the FIVE *toughest* words three times each.

Write a **question** using TWO words.

Write a **quotation** using TWO words.

Write an **exclamation** using TWO words.

What is the *shortest* word?

What is the *longest* word?

Which SEVEN words are the most *interesting*?

Which TWO words are *easiest*?

Describe one **new word** in your own words.

Frequently Misspelled Words: #5

acquaint	hierarchy
aggression	interesting
athletic	library
bicycle	minute
chief	occurrence
destroy	piece
embarrass	prejudice
exciting	quiet
field	relief
guard	search

Frequently Misspelled Words: #5

acquaint	destroy	hierarchy	piece
aggression	embarrass	interesting	prejudice
athletic	exciting	library	quiet
bicycle	field	minute	relief
chief	guard	occurrence	search

Hide the TEN toughest words in this word search

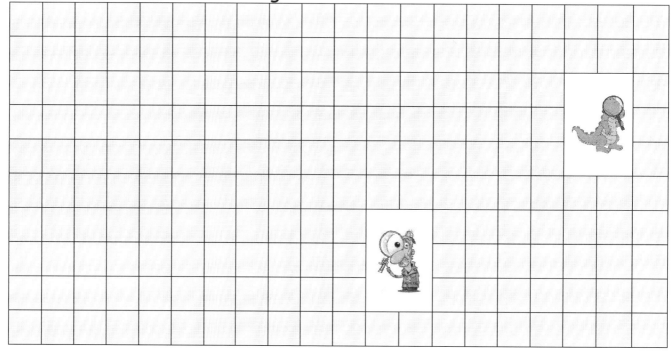

Write a funny story using FIVE of these words.

_____

_____

_____

_____

_____

_____

_____

Frequently Misspelled Words: #5

acquaint	destroy	hierarchy	piece
aggression	embarrass	interesting	prejudice
athletic	exciting	library	quiet
bicycle	field	minute	relief
chief	guard	occurrence	search

Write the TEN **easiest** words once.

Write the FIVE **toughest** words thrice.

Create **questions** (underline your words).

1.

2.

3.

Create **exclamations** (underline your words).

1.

2.

3.

Write three silly sentences using TWO different words in each.

1.

2.

3.

Frequently Misspelled Words: #6

affect	niece
around	parallel
calendar	prairie
criticism	realize
disappoint	restaurant
equipment	secret
forehead	sight
happiness	squirrel
interrupt	themselves
magazine	vacuum

Write the FIVE *toughest* words three times each.

Write a **question** using TWO words.

Write a **quotation** using TWO words.

What is the *shortest* word?

What is the *longest* word?

Write an **exclamation** using TWO words.

Which SEVEN words are the most *interesting*?

Which TWO words are *easiest*?

Describe one **new word** in your own words.

Frequently Misspelled Words: #6

affect   niece

around   parallel

calendar   prairie

criticism   realize

disappoint   restaurant

equipment   secret

forehead   sight

happiness   squirrel

interrupt   themselves

magazine   vacuum

Frequently Misspelled Words: #6

affect	equipment	niece	secret
around	forehead	parallel	sight
calendar	happiness	prairie	squirrel
criticism	interrupt	realize	themselves
disappoint	magazine	restaurant	vacuum

Hide the TEN toughest words in this word search

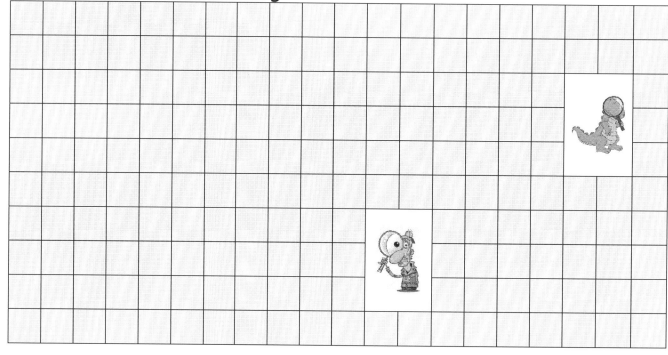

Write a funny story using FIVE of these words.

_____

_____

_____

_____

_____

_____

_____

Frequently Misspelled Words: #6

affect	equipment	niece	secret
around	forehead	parallel	sight
calendar	happiness	prairie	squirrel
criticism	interrupt	realize	themselves
disappoint	magazine	restaurant	vacuum

Write the TEN **easiest** words once.

Write the FIVE **toughest** words thrice.

Create **questions** (<u>underline</u> your words).

1.

2.

3.

Create **exclamations** (<u>underline</u> your words).

1.

2.

3.

Write three silly sentences using TWO different words in each.

1.

2.

3.

Frequently Misspelled Words: #7

across	innocent
always	maneuver
atheist	millennium
captain	omitted
Christian	possession
courteous	questionnaire
does	religion
excellence	sponsor
formerly	temperament
grateful	village

Write the FIVE *toughest* words three times each.

Write a **question** using TWO words.

Write a **quotation** using TWO words.

Write an **exclamation** using TWO words.

Which TWO words are *easiest*?

What is the *shortest* word?

What is the *longest* word?

Which SEVEN words are the most *interesting*?

Describe one **new word** in your own words.

Frequently Misspelled Words: #7

across	innocent
always	maneuver
atheist	millennium
captain	omitted
Christian	possession
courteous	questionnaire
does	religion
excellence	sponsor
formerly	temperament
grateful	village

Frequently Misspelled Words: #7

across	courteous	innocent	questionnaire
always	does	maneuver	religion
atheist	excellence	millennium	sponsor
captain	formerly	omitted	temperament
Christian	grateful	possession	village

Hide the TEN toughest words in this word search

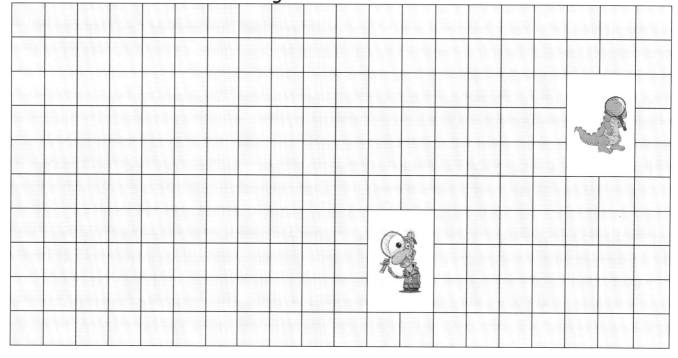

Write a funny story using FIVE of these words.

_____

_____

_____

_____

_____

_____

_____

Frequently Misspelled Words: #7

across	courteous	innocent	questionnaire
always	does	maneuver	religion
atheist	excellence	millennium	sponsor
captain	formerly	omitted	temperament
Christian	grateful	possession	village

Write the TEN **easiest** words once.

Write the FIVE **toughest** words thrice.

Create **questions** (<u>underline</u> your words).

1.

2.

3.

Create **exclamations** (<u>underline</u> your words).

1.

2.

3.

Write three silly sentences using TWO different words in each.

1.

2.

3.

Frequently Misspelled Words: #8

achieve	fourth
already	height
benefit	humorous
choose	knew
continuous	mountain
description	opposite
disappear	privilege
environment	receive
everyone	scenes
finally	thorough

Write the FIVE *toughest* words three times each.

Write a **question** using TWO words.

Write a **quotation** using TWO words.

What is the *shortest* word?

What is the *longest* word?

Write an **exclamation** using TWO words.

Which TWO words are *easiest*?

Which SEVEN words are the most *interesting*?

Describe one **new word** in your own words.

Frequently Misspelled Words: #8

achieve	fourth
already	height
benefit	humorous
choose	knew
continuous	mountain
description	opposite
disappear	privilege
environment	receive
everyone	scenes
finally	thorough

Frequently Misspelled Words: #8

achieve	description	fourth	opposite
already	disappear	height	privilege
benefit	environment	humorous	receive
choose	everyone	knew	scenes
continuous	finally	mountain	thorough

Hide the TEN toughest words in this word search

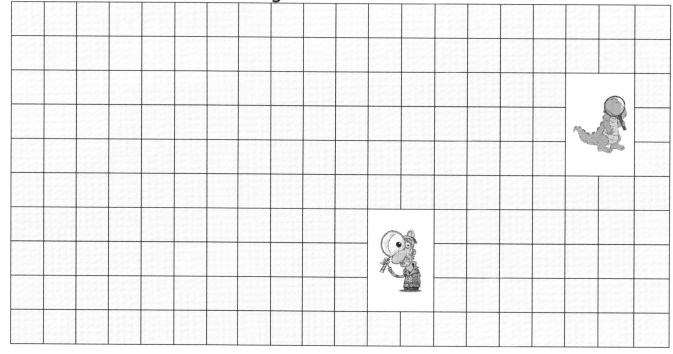

Write a funny story using FIVE of these words.

_____

_____

_____

_____

_____

_____

_____

_____

Frequently Misspelled Words: #8

achieve	description	fourth	opposite
already	disappear	height	privilege
benefit	environment	humorous	receive
choose	everyone	knew	scenes
continuous	finally	mountain	thorough

Write the TEN **easiest** words once.

Write the FIVE **toughest** words thrice.

Create **questions** (<u>underline</u> your words).

1.

2.

3.

Create **exclamations** (<u>underline</u> your words).

1.

2.

3.

Write three silly sentences using TWO different words in each.

1.

2.

3.

Frequently Misspelled Words: #9

approach	quite
author	really
career	rhyme
it's	servant
kernel	speak
laboratory	success
marriage	swimming
narration	usual
preparation	whether
profession	woman

Write the FIVE *toughest* words three times each.

Write a **question** using TWO words.

Write a **quotation** using TWO words.

Write an **exclamation** using TWO words.

What is the *shortest* word?

What is the *longest* word?

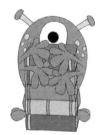

Which SEVEN words are the most *interesting*?

Which TWO words are *easiest*?

Describe one **new word** in your own words.

Frequently Misspelled Words: #9

approach	quite
author	really
career	rhyme
it's	servant
kernel	speak
laboratory	success
marriage	swimming
narration	usual
preparation	whether
profession	woman

Frequently Misspelled Words: #9

approach	laboratory	quite	success
author	marriage	really	swimming
career	narration	rhyme	usual
it's	preparation	servant	whether
kernel	profession	speak	woman

Hide the TEN toughest words in this word search

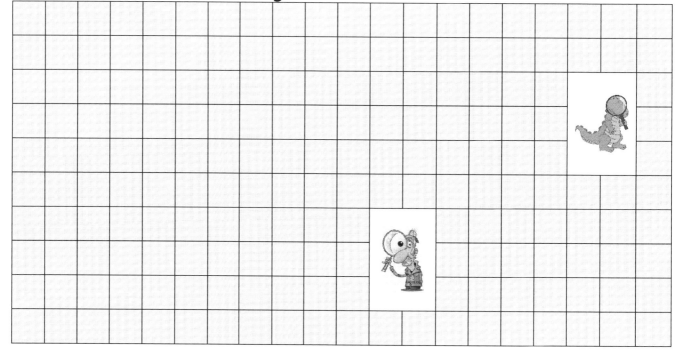

Write a funny story using FIVE of these words.

Frequently Misspelled Words: #9

approach	laboratory	quite	success
author	marriage	really	swimming
career	narration	rhyme	usual
it's	preparation	servant	whether
kernel	profession	speak	woman

Write the TEN **easiest** words once.

Write the FIVE **toughest** words thrice.

Create **questions** (<u>underline</u> your words).

1.

2.

3.

Create **exclamations** (<u>underline</u> your words).

1.

2.

3.

Write three silly sentences using TWO different words in each.

1.

2.

3.

Frequently Misspelled Words: #10

acquire	pleasant
again	pamphlet
conscientious	parents
deceive	procedure
different	reference
easily	seize
excited	surprise
favorite	trouble
noticeable	weather
opportunity	whose

Write the FIVE *toughest* words three times each.

Write a **question** using TWO words.

Write a **quotation** using TWO words.

Write an **exclamation** using TWO words.

What is the *shortest* word?

What is the *longest* word?

Which SEVEN words are the most *interesting*?

Which TWO words are *easiest*?

Describe one **new word** in your own words.

acquire	pleasant
again	pamphlet
conscientious	parents
deceive	procedure
different	reference
easily	seize
excited	surprise
favorite	trouble
noticeable	weather
opportunity	whose

Frequently Misspelled Words: #10

acquire	easily	pleasant	seize
again	excited	pamphlet	surprise
conscientious	favorite	parents	trouble
deceive	noticeable	procedure	weather
different	opportunity	reference	whose

Hide the TEN toughest words in this word search

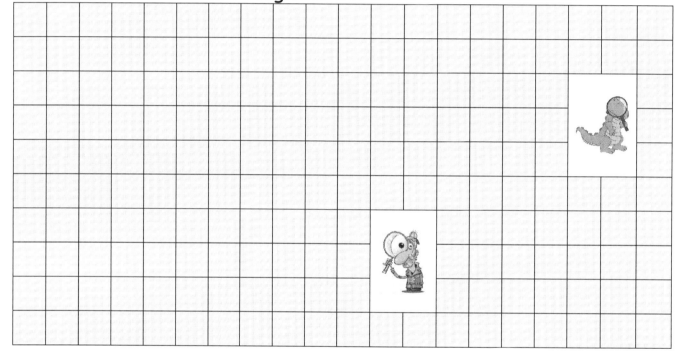

Write a funny story using FIVE of these words.

_____

_____

_____

_____

_____

_____

Frequently Misspelled Words: #10

acquire	easily	pleasant	seize
again	excited	pamphlet	surprise
conscientious	favorite	parents	trouble
deceive	noticeable	procedure	weather
different	opportunity	reference	whose

Write the TEN **easiest** words once.

Write the FIVE **toughest** words thrice.

Create **questions** (<u>underline</u> your words).

1.

2.

3.

Create **exclamations** (<u>underline</u> your words).

1.

2.

3.

Write three silly sentences using TWO different words in each.

1.

2.

3.

Frequently Misspelled Words: #11

against	harass
believe	immediate
brilliant	judgment
collectible	literature
concentrate	misspell
describe	occasionally
discuss	permanent
equipped	prophecy
etc.	schedule
families	stretch

Write the FIVE *toughest* words three times each.

Write a **question** using TWO words.

What is the *shortest* word?

What is the *longest* word?

Write a **quotation** using TWO words.

Write an **exclamation** using TWO words.

Which SEVEN words are the most *interesting*?

Which TWO words are *easiest*?

Describe one **new word** in your own words.

Frequently Misspelled Words: #11

against	harass
believe	immediate
brilliant	judgment
collectible	literature
concentrate	misspell
describe	occasionally
discuss	permanent
equipped	prophecy
etc.	schedule
families	stretch

Frequently Misspelled Words: #11

against	describe	harass	occasionally
believe	discuss	immediate	permanent
brilliant	equipped	judgment	prophecy
collectible	etc.	literature	schedule
concentrate	families	misspell	stretch

Hide the TEN toughest words in this word search

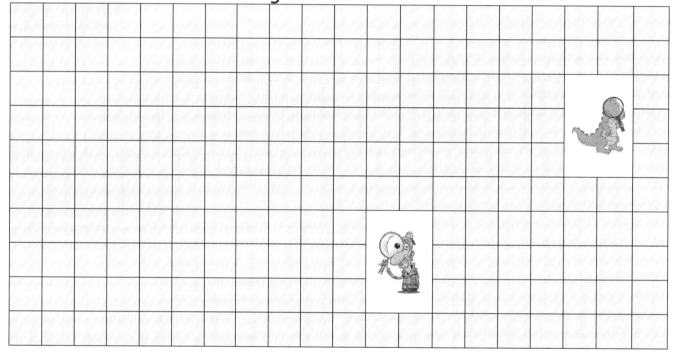

Write a funny story using FIVE of these words.

_____

_____

_____

_____

_____

_____

_____

Frequently Misspelled Words: #11

against	describe	harass	occasionally
believe	discuss	immediate	permanent
brilliant	equipped	judgment	prophecy
collectible	etc.	literature	schedule
concentrate	families	misspell	stretch

Write the TEN **easiest** words once.

Write the FIVE **toughest** words thrice.

Create **questions** (<u>underline</u> your words).

1.

2.

3.

Create **exclamations** (<u>underline</u> your words).

1.

2.

3.

Write three silly sentences using TWO different words in each.

1.

2.

3.

Frequently Misspelled Words: #12

appreciate	particular
apology	possess
apparent	publicly
disease	relieve
immensely	sentence
jewelry	stopped
license	there
loose	thought
nineteen	wait
opinion	writing

Write the FIVE *toughest* words three times each.

Write a **question** using TWO words.

Write a **quotation** using TWO words.

Write an **exclamation** using TWO words.

Which TWO words are *easiest?*

What is the *shortest* word?

What is the *longest* word?

Which SEVEN words are the most *interesting?*

Describe one **new word** in your own words.

Frequently Misspelled Words: #12

appreciate	particular
apology	possess
apparent	publicly
disease	relieve
immensely	sentence
jewelry	stopped
license	there
loose	thought
nineteen	wait
opinion	writing

Frequently Misspelled Words: #12

appreciate	jewelry	particular	stopped
apology	license	possess	there
apparent	loose	publicly	thought
disease	nineteen	relieve	wait
immensely	opinion	sentence	writing

Hide the TEN toughest words in this word search

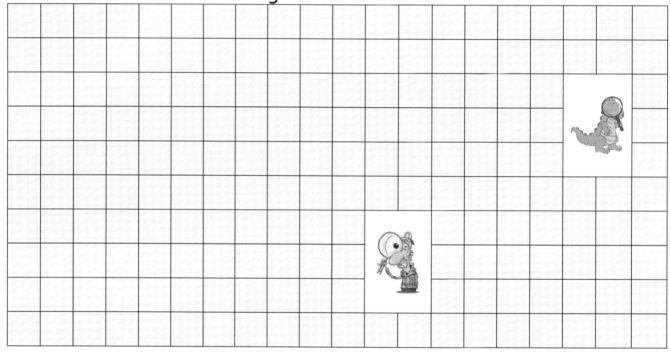

Write a funny story using FIVE of these words.

_____

_____

_____

_____

_____

_____

_____

Frequently Misspelled Words: #12

appreciate	jewelry	particular	stopped
apology	license	possess	there
apparent	loose	publicly	thought
disease	nineteen	relieve	wait
immensely	opinion	sentence	writing

Write the TEN **easiest** words once.

Write the FIVE **toughest** words thrice.

Create **questions** (underline your words).

1.

2.

3.

Create **exclamations** (underline your words).

1.

2.

3.

Write three silly sentences using TWO different words in each.

1.

2.

3.

Frequently Misspelled Words: #13

associate	lonely
beginning	pilot
column	principle
criticize	receipt
descriptive	secretary
exaggerate	summarize
forearm	think
grammar	tried
independence	where
jealous	wreck

Write the FIVE *toughest* words three times each.

Write a **question** using TWO words.

Write a **quotation** using TWO words.

Write an **exclamation** using TWO words.

Which TWO words are *easiest*?

What is the *shortest* word?

What is the *longest* word?

Which SEVEN words are the most *interesting*?

Describe one **new word** in your own words.

Frequently Misspelled Words: #13

associate	lonely
beginning	pilot
column	principle
criticize	receipt
descriptive	secretary
exaggerate	summarize
forearm	think
grammar	tried
independence	where
jealous	wreck

Frequently Misspelled Words: #13

associate	**exaggerate**	**lonely**	**summarize**
beginning	**forearm**	**pilot**	**think**
column	**grammar**	**principle**	**tried**
criticize	**independence**	**receipt**	**where**
descriptive	**jealous**	**secretary**	**wreck**

Hide the TEN toughest words in this word search

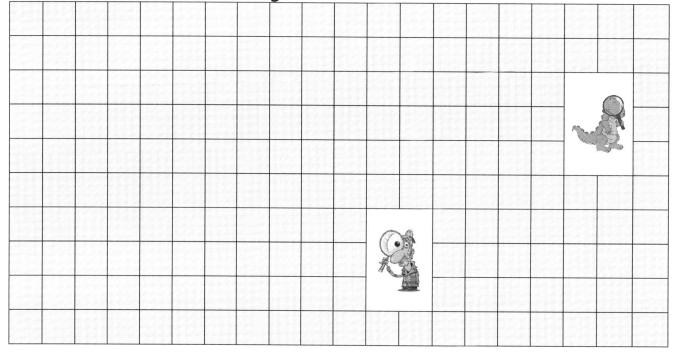

Write a funny story using FIVE of these words.

_____

_____

_____

_____

_____

_____

_____

_____

Frequently Misspelled Words: #13

associate	exaggerate	lonely	summarize
beginning	forearm	pilot	think
column	grammar	principle	tried
criticize	independence	receipt	where
descriptive	jealous	secretary	wreck

Write the TEN **easiest** words once.

Write the FIVE **toughest** words thrice.

Create **questions** (<u>underline</u> your words).

1.

2.

3.

Create **exclamations** (<u>underline</u> your words).

1.

2.

3.

Write three silly sentences using TWO different words in each.

1.

2.

3.

Frequently Misspelled Words: #14

aggressive	indispensable
appreciation	intelligence
awful	miniature
challenge	occurs
conscious	personnel
convenient	principal
difficult	pursuit
everybody	sincerely
fascinate	they're
governor	usually

Write the FIVE *toughest* words three times each.

Write a **question** using TWO words.

What is the *shortest* word?

What is the *longest* word?

Write a **quotation** using TWO words.

Write an **exclamation** using TWO words.

Which SEVEN words are the most *interesting*?

Which TWO words are *easiest*?

Describe one **new word** in your own words.

Frequently Misspelled Words: #14

aggressive	indispensable
appreciation	intelligence
awful	miniature
challenge	occurs
conscious	personnel
convenient	principal
difficult	pursuit
everybody	sincerely
fascinate	they're
governor	usually

Frequently Misspelled Words: #14

aggressive	convenient	indispensable	principal
appreciation	difficult	intelligence	pursuit
awful	everybody	miniature	sincerely
challenge	fascinate	occurs	they're
conscious	governor	personnel	usually

Write the TEN **easiest** words once.

Write the FIVE **toughest** words thrice.

Create questions (<u>underline</u> your words).

1.

2.

3.

Create exclamations (<u>underline</u> your words).

1.

2.

3.

Write three silly sentences using TWO different words in each.

1.

2.

3.

Frequently Misspelled Words: #15

almost	liaison
arctic	medicine
beauty	possessive
character	similar
committee	straight
deceit	thief
existence	together
fiery	truly
government	until
instead	were

Write the FIVE *toughest* words three times each.

Write a **question** using TWO words.

Write a **quotation** using TWO words.

Write an **exclamation** using TWO words.

What is the *shortest* word?

What is the *longest* word?

Which SEVEN words are the most *interesting*?

Which TWO words are *easiest*?

Describe one **new word** in your own words.

Frequently Misspelled Words: #15

almost	liaison
arctic	medicine
beauty	possessive
character	similar
committee	straight
deceit	thief
existence	together
fiery	truly
government	until
instead	were

Frequently Misspelled Words: #15

almost	deceit	liaison	thief
arctic	existence	medicine	together
beauty	fiery	possessive	truly
character	government	similar	until
committee	instead	straight	were

Hide the TEN toughest words in this word search

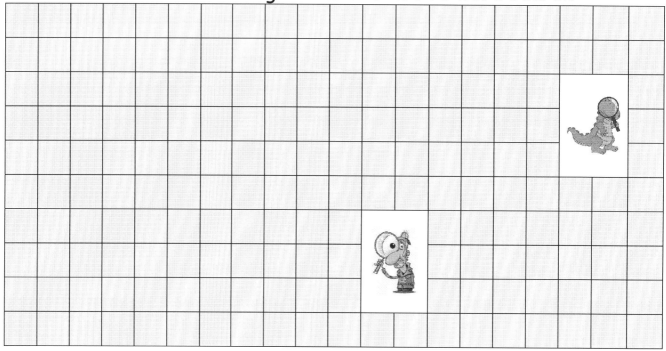

Write a funny story using FIVE of these words.

_____

_____

_____

_____

_____

_____

_____

Frequently Misspelled Words: #15

almost	deceit	liaison	thief
arctic	existence	medicine	together
beauty	fiery	possessive	truly
character	government	similar	until
committee	instead	straight	were

Write the TEN **easiest** words once.

Write the FIVE **toughest** words thrice.

Create **questions** (underline your words).

1.

2.

3.

Create **exclamations** (underline your words).

1.

2.

3.

Write three silly sentences using TWO different words in each.

1.

2.

3.

Frequently Misspelled Words: #16

accuse	independent
answer	lightning
athlete	necessary
certain	persuade
college	probably
convenience	relevant
didn't	succeed
doctor	thoroughly
entertain	women
hospital	written

Write the FIVE *toughest* words three times each.

Write a question using TWO words.

Write a quotation using TWO words.

Write an exclamation using TWO words.

What is the *shortest* word?

What is the *longest* word?

Which SEVEN words are the most *interesting*?

Which TWO words are *easiest*?

Describe one **new word** in your own words.

accuse	independent
answer	lightning
athlete	necessary
certain	persuade
college	probably
convenience	relevant
didn't	succeed
doctor	thoroughly
entertain	women
hospital	written

Frequently Misspelled Words: #16

accuse	convenience	independent	relevant
answer	didn't	lightning	succeed
athlete	doctor	necessary	thoroughly
certain	entertain	persuade	women
college	hospital	probably	written

Hide the TEN toughest words in this word search

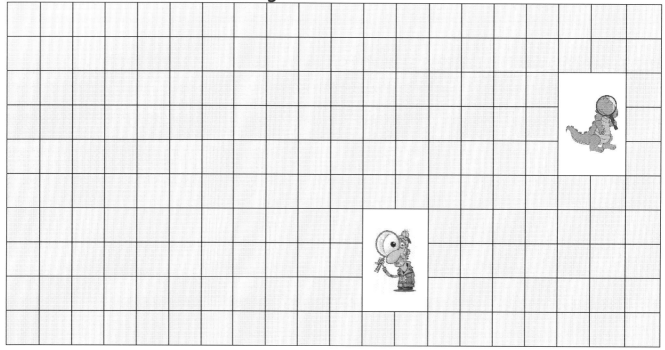

Write a funny story using FIVE of these words.

_____

_____

_____

_____

_____

_____

_____

Frequently Misspelled Words: #16

accuse	convenience	independent	relevant
answer	didn't	lightning	succeed
athlete	doctor	necessary	thoroughly
certain	entertain	persuade	women
college	hospital	probably	written

Write the TEN **easiest** words once.

Write the FIVE **toughest** words thrice.

Create questions (<u>underline</u> your words).

1.

2.

3.

Create exclamations (<u>underline</u> your words).

1.

2.

3.

Write three silly sentences using TWO different words in each.

1.

2.

3.

Frequently Misspelled Words: #17

attitude	minuscule
before	occasion
clothes	practically
decision	psychologist
discussion	repetition
extremely	separate
forest	speech
hoping	summary
incident	those
its	which

Write the FIVE *toughest* words three times each.

Write a **question** using TWO words.

What is the *shortest* word?

What is the *longest* word?

Write a **quotation** using TWO words.

Write an **exclamation** using TWO words.

Which SEVEN words are the most *interesting*?

Which TWO words are *easiest*?

Describe one **new word** in your own words.

attitude	minuscule
before	occasion
clothes	practically
decision	psychologist
discussion	repetition
extremely	separate
forest	speech
hoping	summary
incident	those
its	which

Frequently Misspelled Words: #17

attitude	extremely	minuscule	separate
before	forest	occasion	speech
clothes	hoping	practically	summary
decision	incident	psychologist	those
discussion	its	repetition	which

Hide the TEN toughest words in this word search

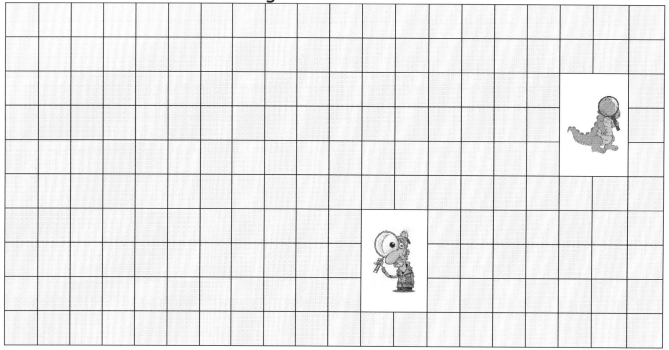

Write a funny story using FIVE of these words.

_____

_____

_____

_____

_____

_____

_____

Frequently Misspelled Words: #17

attitude	extremely	minuscule	separate
before	forest	occasion	speech
clothes	hoping	practically	summary
decision	incident	psychologist	those
discussion	its	repetition	which

Write the TEN **easiest** words once.

Write the FIVE **toughest** words thrice.

Create **questions** (<u>underline</u> your words).

1.

2.

3.

Create **exclamations** (<u>underline</u> your words).

1.

2.

3.

Write three silly sentences using TWO different words in each.

1.

2.

3.

Frequently Misspelled Words: #18

attendance	laid
appeared	lose
article	maybe
business	narrative
climb	perseverance
course	poem
definitely	pronunciation
exhilarate	recommend
forty	referred
happier	safety

Write the FIVE *toughest* words three times each.

Write a **question** using TWO words.

What is the *shortest* word?

What is the *longest* word?

Write a **quotation** using TWO words.

Write an **exclamation** using TWO words.

Which SEVEN words are the most *interesting*?

Which TWO words are *easiest*?

Describe one **new word** in your own words.

Frequently Misspelled Words: #18

attendance   laid

appeared   lose

article   maybe

business   narrative

climb   perseverance

course   poem

definitely   pronunciation

exhilarate   recommend

forty   referred

happier   safety

Frequently Misspelled Words: #18

attendance	course	laid	poem
appeared	definitely	lose	pronunciation
article	exhilarate	maybe	recommend
business	forty	narrative	referred
climb	happier	perseverance	safety

Hide the TEN toughest words in this word search

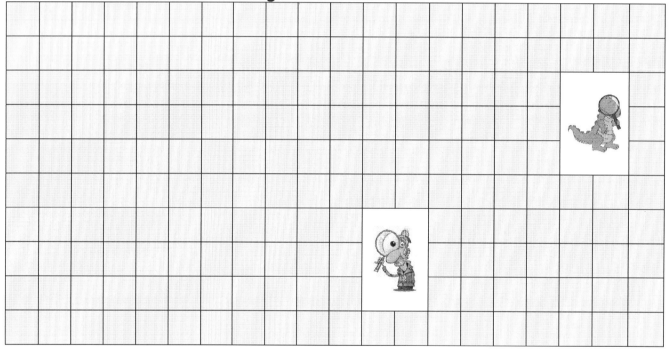

Write a funny story using FIVE of these words.

_____

_____

_____

_____

_____

_____

_____

Frequently Misspelled Words: #18

attendance	course	laid	poem
appeared	definitely	lose	pronunciation
article	exhilarate	maybe	recommend
business	forty	narrative	referred
climb	happier	perseverance	safety

Write the TEN **easiest** words once.

Write the FIVE **toughest** words thrice.

Create **questions** (<u>underline</u> your words).

1.

2.

3.

Create **exclamations** (<u>underline</u> your words).

1.

2.

3.

Write three silly sentences using TWO different words in each.

1.

2.

3.

Frequently Misspelled Words: #19

accept	imagine
accommodate	later
break	paid
descend	precede
drunkenness	recognize
dumbbell	since
enemy	studied
excitement	suspense
first	threshold
foreseen	through

Write the FIVE *toughest* words three times each.

Write a question using TWO words.

Write a quotation using TWO words.

Write an exclamation using TWO words.

Which TWO words are *easiest*?

What is the *shortest* word?

What is the *longest* word?

Which SEVEN words are the most *interesting*?

Describe one **new word** in your own words.

Frequently Misspelled Words: #19

accept	imagine
accommodate	later
break	paid
descend	precede
drunkenness	recognize
dumbbell	since
enemy	studied
excitement	suspense
first	threshold
foreseen	through

Frequently Misspelled Words: #19

accept	dumbbell	imagine	since
accommodate	enemy	later	studied
break	excitement	paid	suspense
descend	first	precede	threshold
drunkenness	foreseen	recognize	through

Hide the TEN toughest words in this word search

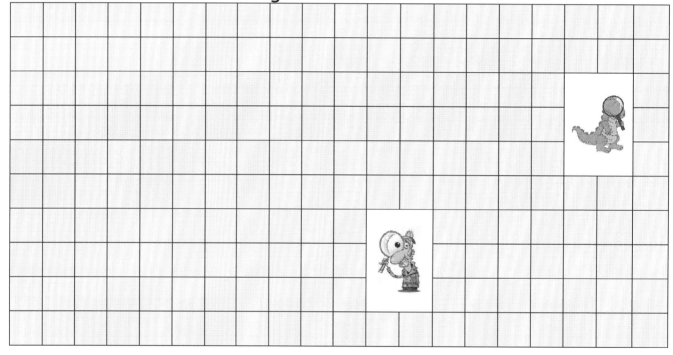

Write a funny story using FIVE of these words.

_____

_____

_____

_____

_____

_____

_____

Frequently Misspelled Words: #19

accept	dumbbell	imagine	since
accommodate	enemy	later	studied
break	excitement	paid	suspense
descend	first	precede	threshold
drunkenness	foreseen	recognize	through

Write the TEN **easiest** words once.

Write the FIVE **toughest** words thrice.

Create **questions** (<u>underline</u> your words).

1.

2.

3.

Create **exclamations** (<u>underline</u> your words).

1.

2.

3.

Write three silly sentences using TWO different words in each.

1.

2.

3.

Frequently Misspelled Words: #20

attendant	inoculate
carrying	medieval
chose	neighbor
consensus	possible
decide	refer
definite	relative
dissatisfy	sense
exceed	suppose
experience	very
humor	writer

Write the FIVE *toughest* words three times each.

Write a **question** using TWO words.

Write a **quotation** using TWO words.

Write an **exclamation** using TWO words.

Which TWO words are *easiest*?

What is the *shortest* word?

What is the *longest* word?

Which SEVEN words are the most *interesting*?

Describe one **new word** in your own words.

Frequently Misspelled Words: #20

attendant	inoculate
carrying	medieval
chose	neighbor
consensus	possible
decide	refer
definite	relative
dissatisfy	sense
exceed	suppose
experience	very
humor	writer

attendant	definite	inoculate	relative
carrying	dissatisfy	medieval	sense
chose	exceed	neighbor	suppose
consensus	experience	possible	very
decide	humor	refer	writer

Hide the TEN toughest words in this word search

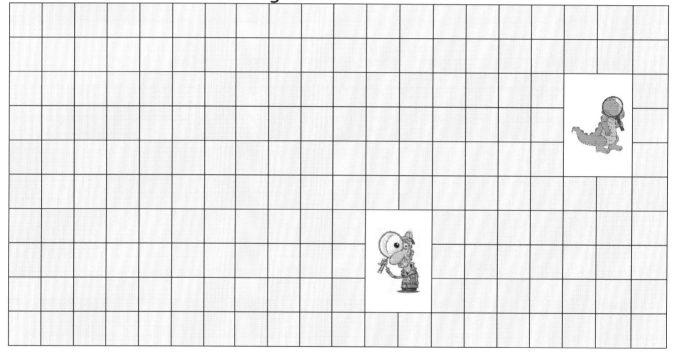

Write a funny story using FIVE of these words.

_____

_____

_____

_____

_____

_____

_____

Frequently Misspelled Words: #20

attendant	definite	inoculate	relative
carrying	dissatisfy	medieval	sense
chose	exceed	neighbor	suppose
consensus	experience	possible	very
decide	humor	refer	writer

Write the TEN **easiest** words once.

Write the FIVE **toughest** words thrice.

Create **questions** (<u>underline</u> your words).

1.

2.

3.

Create **exclamations** (<u>underline</u> your words).

1.

2.

3.

Write three silly sentences using TWO different words in each.

1.

2.

3.

Spelling Quiz

printables

Frequently Misspelled Words

pre-test

1 _____
2 _____
3 _____
4 _____
5 _____
6 _____
7 _____
8 _____
9 _____
10 _____
11 _____
12 _____
13 _____
14 _____
15 _____
16 _____
17 _____
18 _____
19 _____
20 _____

Frequently Misspelled Words

post-test

1 _____
2 _____
3 _____
4 _____
5 _____
6 _____
7 _____
8 _____
9 _____
10 _____
11 _____
12 _____
13 _____
14 _____
15 _____
16 _____
17 _____
18 _____
19 _____
20 _____

Frequently Misspelled Words

Quiz

Practice the words you missed

1 _____

2 _____

3 _____

4 _____

5 _____

6 _____

7 _____

8 _____

9 _____

10 _____

11 _____

12 _____

13 _____

14 _____

15 _____

16 _____

17 _____

18 _____

19 _____

20 _____

I have hundreds of workbooks and activity
books available at Amazon.com

Math

Writing

Spelling

Gifted & Talented

Back to School

Summer

Word Puzzles

Nature & Wildlife

Journals

Activity books

Author: C. Mahoney

Homeschooling Journal
for Gifted and Talented Boys

This homeschool activity book is filled with 100 pages of challenging questions and interesting topics for BOYS. Your son will use the internet to learn about wild animals, airplanes, spiders, teamwork, water sports, games that involve pushing or pulling, the Civil War, Sherlock Holmes, Mount Rushmore, The Boy Scouts, cowboys and the Pony Express. They will investigate the lives of Neil Armstrong, John Muir, John F. Kennedy, Pele, Theodor Seuss Geisel, Ronald Reagan, Vincent van Gogh, Geronimo, Mahatma Gandhi, Elvis Presley and Babe Ruth. They will think about whether it is okay to make fun of other people, how to stay safe near dangerous animals, the differences between a man and a boy, if monsters are real, why men grow beards and mustaches, and why we wear clothes.

This homeschool activity book is filled with 100 pages of challenging questions and interesting topics for GIRLS. Your daughter will use the internet to learn about a nurse's job, sports a girl can play in college, the Girl Scouts, how to become a doctor and which adult jobs are dangerous. They will investigate the lives of Anne Frank, Malala Yousafzai, Mother Teresa, Annie Oakley, Sacagawea, Rosa Parks, Wilma Rudolph, Susan B. Anthony, Queen Nefertiti, Anne Sullivan and Helen Keller. They will think about why reading is important, what makes a woman strong, how a man can show respect to a woman, why boys give girls flowers, how men and women are different, which superpowers a girl might like to have, the jobs available to girls, famous girls in animated movies, why women wear jewelry, why girls like to play with Barbies, how a daughter is different from a mother, is a girl free to love anyone she wants, what is a family, why girls wear dresses and why they tend to have long hair.

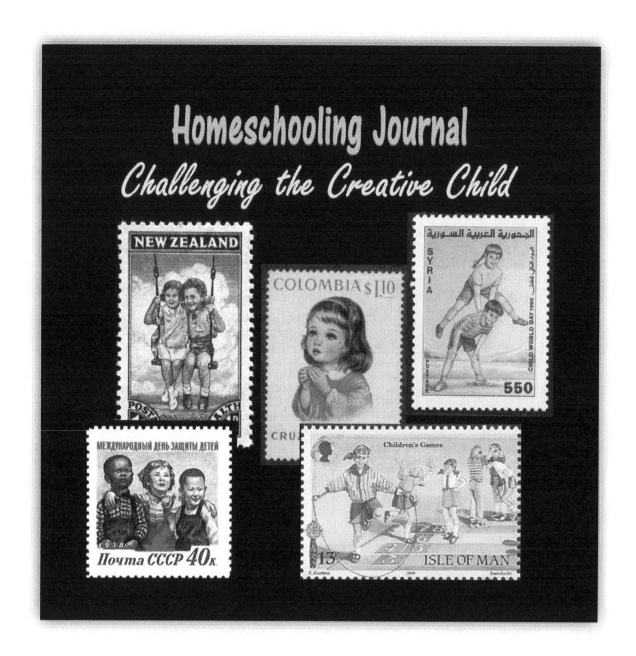

Homeschooling Journal
Challenging the Creative Child

This homeschool JOURNAL is filled with thirty-five international postage stamps and thirty-five thinking activities. Every stamp has an image of a child jumping with friends (Mexico), swinging from a swing (Afghanistan), sewing (Somalia), playing hopscotch (Isle of Man), reading a book (India), writing a letter (Poland), marching (Denmark), sledding on snow (Czech Republic), playing leapfrog (Syria), and more. Explore the customs of other cultures while your child lists their favorite games to play outside, or invents interesting things they can do with a pencil, or thinks up weird jobs they could have as an adult, or lists fun things to do with friends, or imagines things they can stack on a plate, or lists fun things to do in the snow, or thinks about why we wear hats.

Homeschooling Journal
Thinking Outside the Box

This homeschool JOURNAL is filled with forty postage stamps from around the world that lead to forty questions to get your child to think outside the box. Every stamp has an image of a child reading a book (Russia), a child writing (India), a child holding flowers (England), children coloring (Finland), children dancing (Sweden), children playing with string (Australia), children jumping rope (Lebanon), and more. Explore the customs of other cultures while your child lists games they can play with a rope, or describes things they can do with a book (besides read it), or explains when they hold someone's hand, or describes why it is important for a kid to have choices, or lists where they have fallen asleep (other than in a bed), or names animals they have touched with their hand.

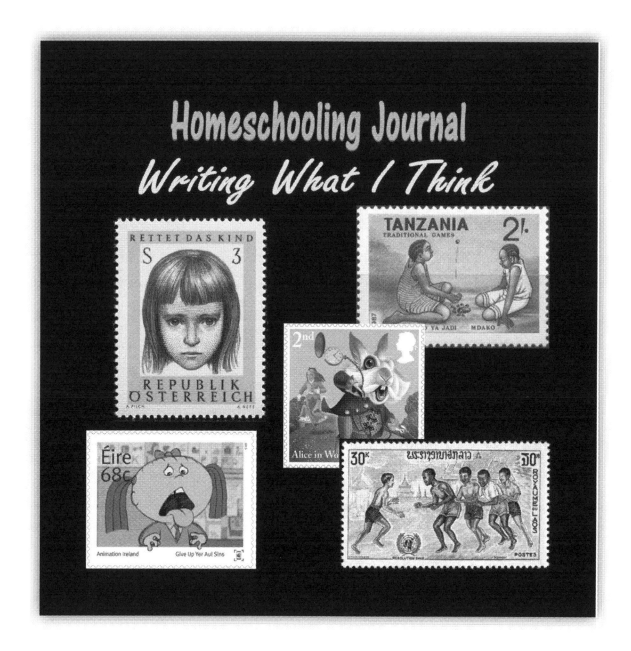

This homeschool JOURNAL is filled with thirty-seven postage stamps from around the world across the page from thirty-seven challenging questions. Every stamp has an image of a child laughing (Belize), reading (Dubai), wrestling (Laos), exercising (Pakistan), sitting with a parent (Kenya), standing beside other kids (Sri Lanka), playing jacks (Tanzania), and more. Explore the customs of other cultures while your child lists fun things to do with snow, or explains why girls wear dresses but boys don't, or lists food or drinks that taste horrible, or writes about why we give gifts, or explains the differences between a child and an adult, or lists things that they can hold in their hand, or thinks about the devices in the home that tell time.

Your child will use the internet to find out which activities require you to hold your breath, how birds learn to fly, how water gets clean, which sports people play on ice, what is in ice-cream, when Christmas was first celebrated and why we give out medals. They will learn about Pegasus, karate, Pecos Bill, Jim Thorpe, what is in the air, water sports, dragons, brightly-colored birds, sports with a hollow ball, Jane Austen, Ted Williams and animals in Antarctica. They will think about whether animals daydream or remember, why people argue, if it is fair to make a horse pull a carriage, how old is too young for someone to work, why people are afraid of certain animals, if it is okay to hit or kick another person, why coins say "In God We Trust," and why adults have to work.

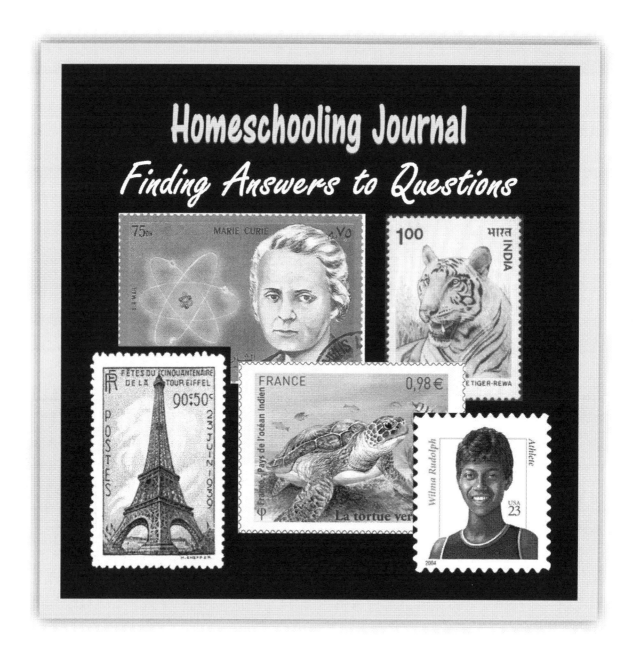

Your child will use the internet to find out how many different ways you can travel, how a scientist learns, how fast a bird can fly, how long a building will last, how little animals defend themselves against bigger animals, how a sailboat works, how safe the ocean is, and how come things taste good. They will learn about George Orwell, Albert Schweitzer, Toni Morrison, Hermann Hesse, Albert Einstein, Herbert Hoover. They will do research on beautiful rocks, fast birds, dangerous animals, penguins, flowers, the Eiffel Tower, bridges, rats, deer and dragons. They will think about whether or not men and women are equal, why people get married, whether or not a woman can do what she wants, if it is okay to shoot someone with a gun, whether or not math is important in life, and if it is okay to put animals in cages in zoos.

Your child will use the internet to find out how metal machines fly in the air, why science is important, how much we learn from vision, how the Teddy bear got its name, where rocks come from, and what is creativity. They will learn about the Nobel Prize, the Statue of Liberty, butterflies, trains, the hummingbird, Cinderlad, satellites, and and stamp collecting. They will do research on Marie Curie, Albert Einstein, Gandhi, Galileo Galilei, Mother Teresa, Benjamin Franklin, Vincent van Gogh, Martin Luther King Jr., and many others. They will think about technology and malaria and driving and Native Americans and nurses and heroes and so much more.

Your child will use the internet to find out how birds learn to fly, what causes waves, what happened to the dinosaurs, and what causes the wind. They will learn about the Girl Scouts, the Great Seal, the Panama Canal, the Supreme Court, Egypt, and the moon. They will do research on Ida B. Wells, Ernest Hemingway, Joan of Arc, Grandma Moses, Elvis Presley, Martin Luther, Abraham Lincoln, Archimedes, St. Nicholas, Benjamin Franklin, and more. They will think about whether or not the circus is fair to animals, whether we have the right to kill other humans (soldiers, police, citizens), whether or not it is important to be pretty, why girls and women wear dresses, whether a doctor is more important than a teacher, what Earth would be like without humans, and more. If you want to develop independence of action, depth of thought, and a curious mind within your homeschooled child, then this is the curriculum choice for you.

Made in the USA
Middletown, DE
08 June 2019